DON'T DO THAT!

A Child's Guide to Bad Manners,
Ridiculous Rules,
and Inadequate Etiquette

by BARRY LOUIS POLISAR

illustrations by David Clark

Table Manners

You are judged by your table manners, so never eat food from the floor—especially if it has been *stepped* on. Remember that it is always a good idea to talk about pleasant things while at the dinner table, so ignore all questions about school.

If you are not sure which piece of silverware to use, it is best to avoid an embarrassing situation by just using your fingers. People have been eating with their fingers for thousands of years and well-educated people know this. Never put your fingers down your throat while eating, however, since gagging at the table is not polite.

Never blow on food to cool it off. If you start to eat a particular food that is too hot, open your mouth widely to cool it off. Stick your tongue out as far as possible and get everyone's attention by pointing to your open mouth and shouting. Insist that everyone look inside.

If a fly or other insect lands on your plate, try to swat it away with your bread. If you are lucky enough to have smashed an insect into your food, pick it up delicately with your thumb and forefinger and place it on the plate of the person sitting next to you.

Proper Ways to Play with Your Food

Although food is meant to be eaten, not played with, there are exceptions. If you *must* play with your food, be creative. You will find that if you make your parents laugh, chances are you will not get in trouble.

Pouring cereal on your head is funny the first few times you do it, but after a while you'll need to come up with something more inventive. Avoid putting carrots up your nose when company is present.

Don't gargle milk, throw crumbs on the floor or pound the table with your fists if you are trying to make a good impression on guests.

Parents play with food all the time. Remember when they used to pretend that a spoonful of mashed potatoes was an airplane and your mouth was the hangar? Pretend your spoonful of mashed potatoes is an airplane on a bombing raid and the floor is filled with bad guys. . . . splatt!!!

New Foods and Ways to Avoid Eating Them

Although many exotic foods are actually quite tasty, most are not. Don't waste your time on asparagus, okra, or succotash. Never eat creamed chipped beef; it tastes exactly the way it looks.

When you dislike the new foods that you sample, always spit them out in a napkin rather than onto the floor or dinner table—especially if you are a guest in someone else's home. Of course, if you should accidentally drop your food, do not say anything and hope no one notices until after you have gone home.

If you do not like the food you are served, do not make your opinion known. Instead, find ways to avoid eating. If you find a hair in your food, announce it loudly. This will alert other diners to the possibility that they too may have hair in their food, and may distract them from making sure that you eat everything on your plate.

It is okay to spit out the following foods: Brussels sprouts, lima beans, liver.

How to Be Excused from the Table

After dinner, lean your chair back away from the table and try to find the center of gravity without actually tipping over. If you find yourself starting to fall, quickly grab the tablecloth and hold on!

Drumming on the table with your silverware is not polite. However, during long, boring conversations, you may drop your spoon repeatedly until your parents tell you to go outside and play. Put up an argument even though that's what you want to do.

Remember: parents like to think they're in charge. It will make them feel good to think they made you leave the table.

Sisters and Brothers

Always try to get along with your brother and sister. It is important to remember that you can't *always* get your way, but you can try.

Do not torture your brother or sister in inappropriate ways. Emotional torture is always the most satisfying—and leaves no evidence!

While your brother or sister is talking on the phone or watching television, sit quietly nearby, making faces. Distort your body into all kinds of positions—but do this without saying a word. If that fails to bother them, imitate their every move; follow them around the house doing everything they do. When they say, "Cut it out!" answer by saying, "Cut what out?"

If you tie your brother or sister to a tree, do not leave them there for more than fifteen minutes.

Never attempt to eat their homework when they are not looking.

In general, follow the golden rule: treat them the way you feel they are treating you.

Getting Along with Adults

Avoid saying things like "It wasn't my fault," especially if it was. Learn to apologize—and use this technique early and often.

Parents love to say "No." Always answer, "Why?" If your parents say, "Because I said so," or "I'm your Mommy, that's why," be aware that they really don't have a reason—or they don't want to take the time to explain things—so ask again. Don't beg or plead, unless you know from previous experience that pleading and begging works if you do it long enough.

When greeting your parents' friends at home, pretend to be gracious. Take their hats and coats and drop them on the floor in the upstairs bedroom. Try on hats and coats for size and look at yourself in your parents' mirror.

Imitate your parents' friends, saying, "Oh, so nice to see you. . . . Lovely weather we are having, isn't it? Your children are so polite." Step on your parents' friends' coats, but do not smash their hats excessively.

Rules for Scaring
Your Grandparents

If you are over thirteen you should refrain from trying to scare your grandparents, since your normal behavior is probably scaring them enough already. Younger children wishing to scare older members of the family do so at their own risk. But if you insist . . . here are the rules:

Never sneak up on Grandma or Grandpa;

Never pretend you are choking or do anything that will upset them (remember: they are not as young as your parents);

Never try to fool them into thinking they have suddenly lost their hearing by mouthing words without saying them out loud;

Never lock yourself in the trunk of their car and start screaming and pounding on the trunk while they are driving down the road.

Taking Trips in the Car

Always insist on sitting by the window; immediately draw an imaginary boundary across the back seat and dare your brother or sister to cross it.

Never let anyone with bad taste pick the radio station and always bring along all your Barry Louis Polisar cassettes. Insist on hearing your favorite tape over and over again until your parents are sick of it and agree to buy you a different one. Never go to the bathroom *before* you get back in the car.

Car trips go by quickly if you complain and whine the whole time. Concentrate on annoying your sister or brother instead of being bored. See how many times you can bother them without getting in trouble, but never call them any of the names you learned at school.

Telephone Manners

Under no circumstances should you allow your babysitter to talk on the phone.

If you are home alone and the phone rings, answer it in the deepest voice you can. Never tell strangers you are home alone; instead, change your voice a few times while you are talking, so the caller thinks there is a party going on. Don't forget to disguise your voice and say, "Are you playing on the phone again?" Answer, "No, Mom." Then hang up quickly.

Never call up famous writers and bother them.

If calls come for your parents, remember to write down all important messages immediately, so you can lose them before they come home.

If the call is a wrong number, pretend you are the person being called. Explain to the caller that you have a bad cold and it has affected your voice. Be creative!

If the phone call is for you and you do not feel like talking, be polite and don't tell the other person that you are bored. Instead, drop the phone repeatedly. Cough and chew gum loudly. Burp if appropriate.

Around the House

It is advisable to put away your toys after you have finished with them, but other things may interfere with your desire to do this. Set aside one day every six to eight months for cleaning your room.

It is a good idea to leave your dirty clothes and towels around for Mom and Dad to pick up, as this makes them feel needed.

You will find that complaining and making faces while brushing your teeth will make the time go by more quickly.

Never giggle when someone says the word "bathroom." There is nothing funny about the word "bathroom." The word "toilet," however, is very funny and may always be laughed at hysterically.

How to Interrupt

Some people like to hear themselves talk and therefore need to be interrupted.

If you decide that what you have to say is more important than what others are talking about, try to interrupt politely with a gentle cough or snort. Escalate to a slight groaning sound. If that fails, begin gagging and gasping for air.

Use only as a last resort: grip throat and scream, *"arrggghhhh!!!"* Fall to the floor, choking. (Note: this device can be used only once per person.)

How to Get Along with Your Teacher

Getting along with your teacher is easy if you follow some simple guidelines. Never wear your underwear on your head at school without a good reason. Never make fun of your teacher by imitating the way he or she talks. Never admit that you forgot to do your homework. Instead, think up funny excuses why you are not prepared. Teachers love to laugh so use this opportunity to show your teacher you are a creative thinker.

If you are called on to answer a question at school, mumble your answer to yourself. When you are writing at your desk, look around frequently to make sure that you are not the only person working.

If your teacher is boring, do not interrupt him or her. Instead, use the time efficiently; begin working on another assignment or close your eyes and rest so you don't fall asleep later when you're home doing something important like watching TV.

What to Do When Your Parents Do Dumb Things

Don't get embarrassed. Instead, look around the room as if you were looking for your *real* parents. . . . When they talk to you, pretend not hear them. If they insist on talking to you, say, "Sorry lady, my Mom said never to talk to strangers" and walk away as quickly as possible. Do not make eye contact with anyone.

Don't yell at your mom or dad because they don't know how to park the car, as this only brings more attention to you. Always carry sunglasses with you and wear them whenever you are with your parents.

Your parents want you to think they are just like everybody else—but you know from living with them that they are definitely weirder than average.

Disturbing Others: How to Do It Successfully

The key to disturbing others depends on who you are disturbing. What bothers some people may not bother others. Brothers and sisters, of course, are the easiest to disturb.

A library or movie theatre is the perfect place for disturbing others. Whispering or singing quietly to yourself is a proven technique, as is rattling candy wrappers and announcing what will happen next in the movie. Always try to disturb those who are seeking total quiet; it is time they realized that the world is not a perfect place.

Disturbing others can be done best in a confined space such as an airplane or bus. Encourage your baby brother to poke at the person you are sitting next to. He can get away with this because he is little. Drooling is also very effective.

Nose Etiquette

There are proper and improper times to pick your nose. The rules are simple:

Never pick your nose while eating.
Never pick your nose when you are anywhere that requires
   being dressed up.
Never pick your nose when anyone is watching.

When you see someone picking his nose while driving, do not point at him. (It's not polite to point!) You may, however, imitate his behavior in an exaggerated way as you drive by, with your face pressed up against the window. It is important to hang your tongue out of your mouth and cross your eyes as you do this.

Never say the word "mucus" in public.